OXFO

Ghos

Prepare to be frightened by these terrifying tales from around Oxfordshire

By

Richard Holland

BRADWELL
BOOKS

Published by Bradwell Books
9 Orgreave Close Sheffield S13 9NP
Email: books@bradwellbooks.co.uk

© Richard Holland 2013

British Library Cataloguing in Publication Data: a catalogue
record for this book is available from the British Library.

1st Edition
ISBN: 9781902674735

Print: Gomer Press, Llandysul, Ceredigion SA44 4JL

Design by:jenksdesign@yahoo.co.uk

Picture Credits: Joe McIntyre, Simon Middleton, ShutterStock
and Richard Holland

CONTENTS

INTRODUCTION

I spent the first ten years of my life in Oxfordshire, in a village beside the Thames near Wallingford. I later moved to North Wales, where my fascination with ghosts was initially inspired by a personal experience of poltergeist activity and then developed as I began to discover the rich folklore of that part of the UK.

It has been enormously interesting to return to my childhood roots and explore Oxfordshire again; the county and its ghost-lore. I have a fond appreciation of its golden cornfields, the subtle billowing of its chalk downs and the beauty of its towns and villages. The western side of the county is part of the Cotswolds Area of Outstanding Natural Beauty. Here the mellow warmth of the Cotswold Stone adds an additional charm to the county's cottages and churches.

Fortunately for the purposes of this book, however, Oxfordshire is not just a pretty place – it has a darker side. It boasts ghost stories galore. This is especially true in Oxford itself and in its ancient University colleges in particular. Here can be found ghostly dons and students – some of them famous – and a plethora of phantom monks whose presence recalls the religious origins of the colleges. A good many of the city's ghosts, and indeed of the wider county, have stories dating back to the Civil War of the 17th century. Oxford became temporarily the headquarters of the monarchy after London was claimed by the Parliamentarians during this turbulent time. No less a figure than King Charles I haunts a number of sites.

Oxfordshire boasts a number of magnificent stately homes, many still in private hands, and a goodly number are haunted. They include one of England's grandest homes, Blenheim Palace, which replaced the historically significant Woodstock Manor. Both Blenheim and Woodstock have experienced ghostly activity. Stonor Park – claimed by more than one authority as England's most beautifully situated country house – also has several ghosts and so too does Minster Lovell Hall, a ruined mansion as eerie as it is romantic. All those open to the public are well worth a visit for more than just their haunted reputations.

Inns and hotels are commonly met with in British ghost-lore. Often they are among the oldest buildings in a community and have therefore seen a great deal of life (and death). Oxfordshire has more than its fair share of haunted hostelries. The ghosts haunting them include such disparate characters as highwaymen and lepers, as well as a number of phantom women, many of whom have tragic histories.

Women feature particularly strongly in Oxfordshire's ghost stories. They include a king's mistress, a queen's rival, a notorious poisoner and 'a Martyr to Excessive Sensibility'. Their stories are all to be found in this book.

I encourage you to explore for yourself not only Oxfordshire's remarkable ghost-lore but also the many attractions of its towns, villages and countryside. You should find that tracking down the spooky sites will introduce you to many other beautiful and fascinating places. But beware – Oxfordshire's roads are also haunted. You will have to have your wits about you as you go on your travels, for ghostly pedestrians, bicycles, coaches and cars all have the habit of abruptly appearing in front of modern motorists.

Richard Holland

A view over Oxford, including Brasenose and Exeter Colleges. Many of Oxfordshire's ghosts are packed into the historic colleges of Oxford University.
Skowronek/ShutterStock

THE OXFORD COLLEGES

Oxford is the UK's oldest university and its colleges are steeped in history. Several are very old indeed, founded in the 13th century. The earliest colleges began as monastic establishments. The conglomeration of these formed the foundations of the university as we know it today. As the reputation of the early colleges grew, more and more scholars flocked to the city and in response more colleges were founded by wealthy patrons. In the 15th century the townsfolk got fed up with all these students (a problem faced by students everywhere to this day!) and chased many of them out. They found shelter in Cambridge, leading to the creation of England's second university. With centuries of continual occupation and so many strong and memorable personalities spending their lives here, it's no surprise to learn the Oxford Colleges have a haunted reputation.

One of the oldest colleges is **Merton College**, founded in 1264. Its ghost dates from the 17th century, a dashing Cavalier by the name of Colonel Francis Windebank. He has been seen inside the college, apparently walking around on his knees because the floor level has been raised since his time. Some years ago a woman encountered him outside the college in the evocatively named Dead Man's Walk (which centuries ago was a path used by medieval Jews to bury their dead). She had not heard of the ghost and assumed he was a living, but oddly dressed, man. She reported:

'He was dressed in a very old-fashioned manner as if he were off to a fancy dress ball. He wore knee-length leather boots, a tunic which was unbuttoned to expose the chest and a hat complete with plumes. He was staring at me in what I thought was an insolent manner. I felt suddenly afraid. I looked at the man and began to reassess his insolence. He was not really staring at me, his eyes were focused beyond me, as if he were waiting for something, and he looked abysmally sad.'

The woman's pet dog took fright at the apparition and ran away, so she went after it. Taking a quick look over her shoulder, she saw the man had turned so that his back was to the wall of the college. Returning home and relating her adventure, one of her student lodgers apprised her of the story of Colonel Windebank. Windebank had failed to secure Bletchingdon House, an Oxfordshire mansion, against Oliver Cromwell's troops during the Civil War, some say because he feared for the safety of his wife and guests in the house. He returned to Oxford, which had become King Charles I's temporary capital, to report what had happened and was promptly shot for cowardice, up against the wall of Merton College. An alternative tradition current in Oxford is that he was shot by Cromwell's men in the Fellows' Garden and this is also pointed out as one of his haunts.

*Dead Man's Walk runs past Merton College, between the college buildings
and the playing field. It is haunted by a Cavalier executed for cowardice.*
Olaf Speier/ShutterStock

A contemporary of Colonel Windebank's haunts **St John's College**. This is William Laud, a former Chancellor of the University and Archbishop of Canterbury. He too stood against Cromwell and was beheaded in the Tower of London in the same year as Windebank, 1645. His body was interred beneath the altar of St John's chapel. His favourite haunt is the library, where, in another similarity with Windebank, he appears to be cut off at the knees, due to a change in the floor level. However, he has a bizarre habit which sets him aside from other ghosts: he enjoys bowling his severed head along the floor!

Archbishop Laud haunts St John's College and enjoys an unusual pastime in the Library.
Doctor Jools/ShutterStock

Ghostly monks haunt **Wadham College**. They probably date from the Augustinian friary that formerly stood here. One of the ghosts is described as a tall, white-cowled figure which is 'a little cloudy'. It has been observed standing by the fireplace in the hall and walking between the hall and the chapel.

John Richardson, author of *Oxford and County Ghost Stories* (J. Hannon and Co. 1977), interviewed Mr Arthur Rees, Head Porter at Wadham in the 1960s, about the sighting of another phantom monk. Mr Rees had just completed one of his regular night patrols and was heading back to his Lodge across the main quad when he felt a chilly gust of wind and a voice whispered in his ear: 'Turn to your right, my good man. Look to your right.' In the moonlight he saw a monk standing in the old doorway to the chapel. He described the figure as wearing a 'black or brown baggy coat, right down to the ground and a hood covering the whole of his head and face'. Its hands were held inside the sleeves as if keeping them warm. The apparition floated towards Mr Rees, keeping close to the wall of the chapel. Although the moonlight was bright, Mr Rees shone his torch at it in the hope of being able to see its face. But instead the beam passed right through the cowl. The monk 'drifted up to the dining hall and vanished'.

Mr Rees informed John Richardson of a number of other strange happenings at Wadham. He said that from time to time 'kicking and banging on the thick wooden gates of the college' beside the Porters' Lodge sent them running out but no one was ever found to account for the disturbance. A weird phenomenon was also experienced in the Lodge itself. They nicknamed it 'the presser'.

'It's like a great weight pressing down on you from above,' explained Mr Rees. 'You can't get up even though you try. The pressure gets greater and greater; it's on your shoulder, your head, your feet and on your chest. It gets so great you can hardly breathe. Then suddenly it goes, you can breathe again.'

More than one ghostly monk has been seen around Wadham College.
Doctor Jools/ShutterStock

Obadiah Walker is the ghost of **University College**. Walker was Master of the College during the reign of King James II. He was a staunch supporter of the king and after the Glorious Revolution of 1688, when James II was removed from the throne, he attempted to follow the king to his exile in France. But he was caught and imprisoned by the new regime. Much later he was freed, a broken and embittered man, and lived for just another ten years. He spent that time in his old college, in Room 1, on Staircase 8. His sorrowful spirit is said to still linger in the room.

Magdalen College is haunted by two other tragic figures. One is playwright Oscar Wilde, who was a student here in the 1870s. The other is George Napier, a Jesuit who was executed for his faith in 1568. Napier's body was quartered, with each part stuck up on display on the four gates into Oxford, his head on the gate at Christ Church. His relatives rescued his body parts under cover of darkness in order to give them a decent burial but they were unable to recover his head. The result, tradition states, is that his ghost is still sorrowfully searching for it. He has been seen up and down the length of Banbury Road and on the road from Oxford to Temple Farm, in the latter case riding comfortably in a spectral coach. His heavy, dragging footsteps have also been heard in his old home, a house which now belongs to Magdalen College. His face has been seen peering through a window here – so either he has at last found his head, or this ghost was of his head only, minus his body!

Also headless is the black shadowy shape which silently glides across a lawn in Magdalen College. It has the unnerving habit of 'keeping pace' with people as they cross the lawn. It is possibly the ghost of a monk.

The apparitions which a Magdalen student said invaded her bedroom in the 1980s were definitely those of monks. The girl was lying in bed recovering from a cold when she heard singing coming from somewhere below her room, situated on the top floor of a building in the Chaplain's Quadrangle. The singing came closer and she realised it was coming up the stairs. She told the press: 'I saw the handle of the door turning. There were a number of figures standing in the doorway dressed in black cowls and black robes. The singing was very loud now and as the door opened a current of air carried a nasty stench into my room.'

This unpleasant smell was made no more bearable by the choking clouds of incense exuding from the censers they were swinging.

'They slowly entered the room singing and swinging their censers,' continued the witness. 'Their hoods were deep and completely covered their faces. They gathered around the bed and bent forward slightly as if to peer down at me through those heavy black hoods. Then they stopped singing. I thought this was the moment that they would all throw back their ghastly hoods, show me who they all were and we would all have a good laugh at the joke.'

Instead they started chanting in Latin. Recognising at last that her visitors were not of this world, the girl screamed and ran from the room, passing through them as if they were mist. Later she repeated some of the chants to a linguistics professor (she had studied Latin herself) and he recognised them as a medieval burial chant for the dead. At the time of the visitation, the student in the room below the witness confirmed hearing singing and heavy footsteps from above. At the time of the sighting, archaeologists were excavating the buried ruins of St John's Hospital, which originally stood on the site of the Chaplain's Quadrangle. It has been suggested the dig may have disturbed the spirits of some of the medieval monks and they had been attracted to the girl's room because she was unwell.

Magdalen is one of Oxford's most haunted colleges.
Irina Korshunova/ShutterStock

A host of phantom black monks allegedly invaded a student's room at Magdalen College and started to pray over her as she lay in bed.
mogen creative/ShutterStock

Excavations were also blamed for the alleged sighting of yet another headless ghost, this time at **Exeter College**. Dr Thomas Wood, later a composer of choral music, claimed to have seen the spook outside his room in Exeter College on Hallowe'en night, 1916. He had just opened the door to his room, which was situated five flights up on Staircase VI, when he was shocked to see a headless and transparent figure standing right outside, its arm raised as if about to knock. The apparition was that of a man wearing a black gown over a buff coat with 'yellow slashings'. These slashings, made to reveal the bright colour of the lining of the coat, might date the ghost to the early 1600s. For several seconds Dr Wood stood aghast and the headless figure stood unmoving – and then vanished. Dr Wood hurtled out of the door and down the five flights of stairs to where his friend was waiting in the stairwell.

The next morning, at a tutorial, Dr Wood learnt that excavations undertaken to enlarge a coal cellar below Staircase VI had uncovered an interesting artefact: a broken statue of some antiquity. Dr Wood got a surprise when he saw it. It was of a man in the fashion of the early 1600s with a gown over a slashed coat, and it was headless. To Dr Wood it seemed as if the apparition of the night before had been a projection of the statue. Research revealed that the statue had been a memorial to a former scholar, John Crocker, and had originally been situated in the old chapel, which was demolished in the 1850s. How it found its way to its new position, in a shattered state, remained a mystery. It was reinstalled in the New Chapel, where it can be seen to this day. The traditional Hallowe'en date given for the sighting and the fact that Dr Wood had been about to attend a meeting of a student society called 'The Unbelievers Club' when he saw the ghost both suggest to me that perhaps Dr Wood's interesting story should be taken with a pinch of salt.

Excavations may have been the cause of two of the ghost stories cited above, but the following account is of a ghost carrying out its own excavation. It was seen one night in 1947 by Mary Ogilvie, wife of the then Principal of **Jesus College**. She was woken by the barking of a college servant's dog – it often annoyed her by barking at night – and she looked out of the window into the Principal's Garden. There she was astonished to see a man, 'dressed rather strangely, wearing a strange hat', digging a hole in her lawn. He'd already excavated one big hole and was starting on another. Mary Ogilvie woke her husband, who grumpily stumped to the window and peered down. The excavator was beginning a third hole. Sir Frederick refused to go down and accost the man, saying he needed his sleep and would sort it out in the morning. His wife reluctantly returned to bed. The next morning the lawn was found to be in perfect condition: nothing had been disturbed.

The Ogilvies later learnt of a tradition that in 1643, during the Civil War, one of King Charles's right-hand men, Viscount Grandison, returned wounded from battle to find his wife with a lover. He immediately challenged the fellow to a duel but, greatly weakened, he was killed. According to the story, he was secretly buried by his faithless wife and lover in the garden below the Ogilvies' window. This might in part explain their strange experience but of course it doesn't explain why at least three holes were dug. Rob Walters, in his *Haunted Oxford* (Tempus 2006), suggests that perhaps the spirit of the lover is continuing to dig up the ground in search of Grandison's body. Of course, it's also possible the apparition had nothing to do with the Grandison story and it dated from a much earlier time. Perhaps corpses were buried in that spot during a period of plague? It remains one of Oxford's more intriguing ghosts.

Another unusual apparition seen at Jesus College was that of a living man. Two students saw one of the dons calmly stroll through a solid wall between the chapel and the dining hall. The man himself was not even in Oxford at the time and quite unaware of his doppelganger.

Queen's College has a more recent apparition in Cuthbert Shields, the name adopted by a clergyman who believed he was the reincarnation of St Cuthbert. His real name was John Laing and he adopted the surname of Shields because he came from South Shields. Although he was a student at Corpus Christi, he spent most of his time in research in Queen's College Library. On his death in 1900 it was found he had left a collection of his papers to the library, sealed up in a tin box. He stipulated that the papers could only be examined fifty years after his death. In 1950, the box was opened to reveal – very little. Inside was an uninspiring pile of handwritten letters to an archdeacon and prophecies for the future which were immediately discounted. Those who had witnessed the opening of the box walked off in disgust and the librarian left it lying on his desk while he busied himself with more important matters.

Later on that night one of his colleagues saw an elderly man with a shock of white hair apparently going through the contents of the box. The librarian began to approach the intruder to ask him his business when he realised he was no longer there. His description was found to tally with that of the self-styled Cuthbert Shields. Shields's apparition has been seen since, roaming the upper library and entering the alcove where his collection of disregarded papers has been filed.

In May 1948, a pair of ghosts was seen by student Miles Hudson in Kettell Hall, one of the oldest parts of **Trinity College**. Mr Hudson had been to a party and was still awake at 3am, his head full of the evening's events as well as alcohol. He was startled to see the apparitions of two men float through his closed and locked door. Only their upper halves were visible; they were without legs. The figures closely resembled each other – they appeared to be twins of about sixty years of age – and were similarly dressed, in clerical collars. They drifted across to where the student lay, looked down at him, smiled, then vanished through a wall.

Mr Hudson wasn't frightened by this experience but he was highly intrigued. He was determined to find out the identities of his unusual visitors. His following investigation proved very interesting. Ultimately he became satisfied that the apparitions were those of twin brothers Noel and Christopher Chavasse, former scholars of Trinity, whose father had founded St Peter's College. Christopher's son was a fellow student of Mr Hudson's, and also had rooms in Kettell Hall – indeed he had had a row with him at the party that same night, which may have been the reason for the visitation.

The really peculiar thing is that one of the twins, Christopher, was dead – he had died in the First World War at the age of thirty – but Noel was still alive, aged sixty-four (in 1948 he was the Bishop of Rochester). So Mr Hudson had not only seen the phantasm of a living man but also of his dead brother, who had aged as he would have done if he had survived the war. Very peculiar! Mr Hudson also learnt that ghostly twins had been seen previously around Kettell Hall, as early as twenty years before. One wonders whether they then appeared aged in their forties, rather than their sixties.

Trinity College is haunted by a pair of ghostly twins.
Ilya D. Gridnev/ShutterStock

New College is said to be haunted by the Reverend William Archibald Spooner, whose muddled use of words gave the world 'Spoonerisms' (much to his own annoyance). His most famous Spoonerisms include an after-dinner toast to 'the queer old Dean' instead of the 'dear old Queen'; suggesting that the 'hags should be flung out' instead of the flags hung out; and accusing two students of 'pissing all his mystery lectures'. Spooner spent most of his adult life at New College, both as a student and as a don. He is described as having been 'an albino, small, with a pink face, poor eyesight and a head too large for his body'. His ghost has therefore been easily recognisable by those who claim to have seen him. Ghost-hunter Ross Andrews, in his book *Paranormal Oxford* (Amberley, 2010), also mentions another ghost at New College. Seen in the chapel, it is described as 'a figure, possibly a priest, with an unnaturally pallid face'. The 'pallid face' suggests, however, that this may also be the albino Revd Spooner.

Hauntings in a couple of other colleges are also mentioned by Ross Andrews. He states that at **All Souls College** an ill-defined, misty white figure has been glimpsed drifting from the rear of the chapel into the library, and that a staircase at **St Edmund Hall** is haunted by the unhappy spirit of a suicide.

An unearthly misty shape has been seen drifting round All Souls College.
Stanley Loong/ShutterStock

King Charles I has also allegedly been seen at **Christ Church College**. In common with so many Oxford ghosts, he is sometimes minus his head. The chapel of Christ Church College doubles up as England's smallest cathedral. In the 1920s something peculiar happened here, spooky enough to deserve a place in this book.

From 1855, Henry Liddell became a long-serving Dean of Christ Church. Dean Liddell had ten children, one of whom unexpectedly became a celebrity when the Revd Charles Dodgson, better known as Lewis Carroll, took a shine to her. Her name was Alice and she became immortalised in Carroll's *Alice's Adventures in Wonderland* and *Through the Looking Glass*. Alice had a sister, Edith, who died young. Edith had been a great favourite with all the family, particularly her father, who was grief-stricken after her death. For years any mention of Edith was banned from the Liddell house because it caused so much distress to the Dean. A memorial plaque to Edith was placed in Christ Church Cathedral, close to a stained-glass window showing the martyrdom of St Catherine for which she had been the model.

After Dean Liddell's death a damp stain appeared on the wall which those who knew him swore looked just like him. The Dean's 'face' in profile gazed sombrely at the plaque dedicated to his beloved daughter. The image remained for many years and its photograph appeared as an interesting enigma in a number of national publications.

*The stain said to resemble Dean Liddell which mysteriously appeared
in Christ Church Cathedral beside the plaque in memorial
to his daughter Edith.*
© R Holland

MORE FROM OXFORD

In **Broad Street** can be found a granite cross inlaid in the street. This commemorates the spot where three of England's most significant church reformers were burned at the stake during the reign of Bloody Mary. They were Thomas Cranmer, Archbishop of Canterbury; Hugh Latimer, Bishop of Worcester; and Nicholas Ridley, Bishop of London. It should not be confused with the far grander Martyrs' Memorial near Balliol College. At the site of the executions, a weird glow has been seen. Some believe this to be a ghostly echo of the blazing pyre that consumed the lives of the three bishops in the 1550s.

In 1995, during an organised ghost walk, a twelve-year-old girl happened to look back here and was startled to see a vision of an execution taking place. Not only was the girl able to describe the pyre but also the Tudor style of the participants' clothes and one other authentic detail – bags of gunpowder tied round the necks of the prisoners.

Eleanor Jourdain, who became Principal of St Hugh's College in 1915, also claimed to have seen visions of Oxford's past. The most striking apparently showed a prisoner of the Middle Ages being carted down **St Margaret's Road**, which was lined with jeering and capering townsfolk. Jourdain is one of the two women (the other being Charlotte Moberly) who announced in their book *An Adventure* (1901) that they had spent an hour or so wandering around the grounds of Versailles, seeing people and events as they were in the 1700s. It would seem Miss Jourdain was rather prone to such 'time slip' experiences!

Oxford Castle was built by the Normans but by the 18th century had become a prison and administrative centre. Parts of the old gaol have been converted into a hotel; the rest are open to the public as the Oxford Castle Unlocked experience. Thanks to its spooky reputation, October and November at the castle is given over to a GhostFest. The former prison became nationally known for paranormal activity in the 1970s when poltergeist activity broke out, allegedly after inmates held a seance. Included in the ghostly goings-on were sightings of vague apparitions by the guards. Several saw a misty shape ascending a staircase and another encountered a shadowy figure which was presumably also seen by his guard dog, for it immediately started growling. The crypt is one of the oldest parts of Oxford Castle and this is the haunt, it is said, of a ghostly monk who wanders about swearing in a manner thoroughly unbecoming in a monk.

Behind the prison is the original castle mound, which later became used as an execution mound. This is one of several places said to be haunted by Mary Blandy, a young woman who was hanged here in the 18th century for murdering her father (see also 'The Story of Mary Blandy' in the next chapter).

The churchyard of Oxford's oldest church, **St Giles'**, is haunted by the quiet ghost of a woman dressed in grey. She is believed to be the restless spirit of a wealthy woman who left a generous bequest to help the poor people of the parish only to have it appropriated by her greedy relatives instead.

*Oxford Castle later became a prison and it is from this period of its life
that most of its ghostly activity dates.*
Stephen Finn/ShutterStock

Another phantom woman has been seen in the cellar of the
Eagle and Child pub further down the thoroughfare of St Giles.
Who she is and why she should haunt such a cramped space is
unknown. The Eagle and Child, incidentally, is famous for being
the meeting place of The Inklings, a group of literary friends
which included the great fantasists J R R Tolkien and C S Lewis.
The street outside is said to occasionally be graced by the
presence of King Charles I, who promenades about just as he
did when he lived in Oxford during the Civil War.

*The ghost of King Charles I has been reported from several sites in Oxford.
During the Civil War, the king moved his court to the town to avoid the
Parliamentarians in London.*
Georgios Kollidas/ShutterStock

The ghost haunting a three-storey Elizabethan townhouse on the corner of the **High Street** and **Magpie Lane** (now part of the Old Bank Hotel) has been identified as Prudence Burcote. Prudence was a Puritan and therefore a supporter of Oliver Cromwell during the Civil War. This was not a safe position to be in during the period when King Charles's court was based here. To make matters worse for Prudence she committed the unthinkable – she fell in love with a Royalist officer, a member of Queen Henrietta's household. Not surprisingly, the love affair ended badly and this is why Prudence's name has been linked with the ghost of the house. However, the description and behaviour of the ghost are at odds with what one would expect of a Puritan woman: she is rather finely dressed, for one thing, and for another, she enjoys pinching glasses of sherry at parties! Dating from the same period is the ghost of Old Marston. Martson was a farmer who found out that his wife was having an affair with one of Cromwell's men and, in a frenzy of jealous rage, dispatched her with an axe. He performed this bloody deed in what is now **Arnold's Way**, just to the west of Oxford, where Matthew Arnold's School stands.

In **New College Lane** the sounds of fierce fighting have been heard. This is thought to be the echo of a skirmish that took place between Roundheads and a party of Cavaliers led by Prince Rupert of the Rhine, King Charles's nephew.

New College Lane still echoes to the sounds of a Civil War battle.
Lee Torrens/ShutterStock

One of Oxford's better-known ghosts is the so-called 'Black Diver of **Magdalen Bridge**'. This rather grand bridge spans the River Cherwell on the eastern approach to town. The 'Black Diver' has been seen standing on the parapet, gesticulating wildly, before suddenly tipping backwards into the river. He is described as small in stature with black skin and a round head and he is wearing a brown coat or gown over a grubby collarless shirt. The story behind this striking little apparition is that he was a chimney sweep who was shot to death during riotous election celebrations in 1754.

After an initial Tory success, the Whigs ultimately won the election after successfully proving the results had been rigged. On the Whig victory being announced, their supporters celebrated with abandon, loudly berating the losers, whose dirty tricks had been exposed in court. An angry gang of disappointed Tories marched up the High Street, more than ready for a fight. One of these was the little sweep, who capered up and down on the parapet hurling abuse at the occupants of a carriage who were struggling to get through the crowd. Nonchalantly, one of the carriage's occupants, a Captain Turton, aimed his pistol out of the window and shot the sweep in mid caper. The crowd was so shocked that the people parted to let the carriage pass.

William Hogarth, the satirical artist, created four prints lampooning the shenanigans surrounding the elections of his time. One of these, *Chairing the Member*, shows the chaos which erupted on the initial Tory victory being announced at Oxford in 1754. On the left of this picture can be seen a little, soot-stained sweep crouching on a gate-post. The ghost of Magdalen Bridge strongly resembles this little fellow and, since the drawing was made on the spot, it might even be the same man.

*Magdalen Bridge over the River Cherwell. The bridge is the haunt of a weird
apparition known as the 'Black Diver'.*
Chris Hawker/ShutterStock

Finally, we must consider the mysterious experience had by a
young man cycling into Oxford in 1899. Ernest Henham was
riding his new bicycle back into town from his home in
Wallingford when he happened to notice the distinctive figure
of Miss Frances Skene crossing the road in front of him. Miss
Skene was a notable personality in Oxford at the time, a well-
known philanthropist and prison reformer, who had often visited
Mr Henham's school when he was a youngster. Pleased to see
her, Mr Henham decided it would be good to say hello, but by
the time he had dismounted, he had lost sight of her in the
crowd.

In 1902 Mr Henham bought a biography of Miss Skene that had just been published and was surprised to read that the date given for her death was October 6, 1899. He felt certain that it was in November 1899 that he last saw Miss Skene. After a rummage, he was able to turn up the receipt for his bike and found it was dated October 3. He clearly remembered that for the first few days after purchasing his bike he had practised riding it: he could not have made that ride from Wallingford to Oxford until some time later, certainly not before Miss Skene had departed this life. And yet he was equally sure it was Miss Skene and no one else he had seen that day. Mr Henham concluded that the only explanation was that he had seen her ghost.

William Hogarth's satirical print of the Oxford election of 1754. The figure of the little sweep crouched above the skull-and-crossbones on the gate-post is similar to the one haunting Magdalen Bridge and may even represent the same person.

THE STORY OF MARY BLANDY

Mary Blandy was executed for murder in 1752. She was the daughter of Francis Blandy, a solicitor who was Town Clerk of **Henley-on-Thames**. Francis was well off and let it be known that his daughter had expectations of a £10,000 inheritance when the time came. This made her one of the more eligible girls in Henley but her lack of good looks, including a smallpox-scarred face, and perhaps a flaw or two in her character – bearing in mind what later transpired – meant suitors were slow to come forward. Then, in 1746, she met Captain William Henry Cranstoun, a guest of a family friend. They hit it off and an understanding grew between them.

The following year Captain Cranstoun declared his love openly and proposed. There was just one problem – he was already married. Francis Blandy was furious at the deception but Cranstoun assured Mary and her mother that he was in the process of getting the marriage annulled. He tried and failed in this but neglected to tell the Blandys the bad news. Cranstoun continued his visits to Mary, thanks to the sympathetic support of her mother. But when Mrs Blandy died in 1749, Mary's father became increasingly hostile towards Cranstoun, actively discouraging his visits.

In August 1751 the story took a more sinister turn. Cranstoun encouraged Mary to slip a 'love philtre' into her father's food and drink, which he said would soften his heart and make him better disposed towards them. This she did – and Francis Blandy immediately became violently ill. Their maid drank a cup of tea intended for Mr Blandy and she became sick, too. One would have thought that by this time Mary would have realised the powder Cranstoun had given her was anything but a love potion. Nevertheless, a few days later, she put some more in her father's gruel. He became so ill from this dose that an apothecary had to be called. A servant who ate some of the leftover gruel was also taken ill. The family cook, now highly suspicious, examined the gruel and found a white powder in the bottom of it.

A final fatal dose of the drug was given by Mary to her father on August 14. As he lay dying, Mary tried to burn the paper containing the remnants of the poison by throwing it on the kitchen fire. Unbeknownst to her, the cook retrieved it. Francis Blandy's last words were of forgiveness for his daughter and a further warning in regards to Cranstoun. Then he breathed his last and Mary left the house and headed for the Angel Inn. Was she meeting someone there? Was she intending to take a coach away from Henley? Was her heart full of triumph or remorse? These questions cannot be answered. Rumours of what was going on at the Blandy house had spread around the town and Mary was prevented from reaching the inn by an angry crowd.

Mary was put on trial, found guilty of murder and hanged at Oxford. She protested her innocence throughout her trial and even on the gallows. To this day people argue over whether Mary Blandy was a cold-hearted poisoner or the naive dupe of a ruthless would-be bigamist.

A drawing of Mary Blandy, made at the time of her execution in 1752.

For many years after her execution, the ghost of Mary Blandy haunted her former home. The house, in Hart Street, was knocked down years ago but her apparition is still said to be seen from time to time in the garden. Her ghost has also been encountered in the countryside round Turville, over the Buckinghamshire border, a place she often visited in life. But her most dramatic ghostly appearances have been, surprisingly enough, on stage. The Kenton Theatre in Henley is a charming old playhouse built in the early 1800s. In 1969 the theatre was staging a play about Mary Blandy by local author Joan Morgan. During rehearsals, the company began to become aware of a series of strange goings-on. As Betty Puttick explains in her *Oxfordshire Stories of the Supernatural* (Countryside 2003):

'Doors would open by themselves, then slam shut suddenly, and lights came on and off without human intervention. Then the cast were aware of the figure of a woman standing at the back of the theatre, apparently watching the rehearsals, but whenever anyone approached her she faded away into the shadows and was gone.'

The play's author, Joan Morgan, recalled that some years previously, when a dramatisation of Mary Blandy's trial was being staged at the Kenton Theatre, the same thing had happened: a mysterious woman in black had lurked in the shadows watching the rehearsals. Was this then the ghost of Mary herself, taking a not unreasonable interest in these portrayals of her life? Members of the cast and crew certainly seemed to think so.

Henley-on-Thames is haunted by the ghost of convicted poisoner
Mary Blandy. The large building visible across the river is the Angel on the
Bridge, the inn to which Mary ran after her father died.
Peter Elvidge/ShutterStock

THE STORY OF SARAH FLETCHER

In 1936 a collection of *True Ghost Stories* was published by two society ladies, the Marchioness Townshend of Raynham and her friend Maude ffoulkes. Several of these stories were first-hand accounts by the authors themselves. In 1913 Mrs ffoulkes was staying in Oxfordshire and idling away a summer's day at **Dorchester**. As she pottered round the graveyard in the town's ancient Abbey Church, she spotted a headstone which bore this remarkable inscription:

'Reader! If thou hast a Heart famed for Tenderness and Pity, Contemplate this Spot, In which are deposited the Remains of a Young Lady whose artless Beauty, innocence of Mind and gentle Manners once obtained her the Love and Esteem of all who knew her. But when Nerves were too delicately spun to bear the rude Shakes and Jostlings which we meet with in this transitory World, Nature gave way. She sunk and died, a Martyr to Excessive Sensibility.'

It was a memorial to a Mrs Sarah Fletcher, who had 'departed this life at the Village of Clifton on the 7th of June 1799 in the 29th year of her age'.

'Spellbound is the exact expression which describes my state of mind as I looked at this pathetic gravestone,' writes Mrs ffoulkes. The vicar, a Revd Poyntz, happened to notice the young woman staring 'spellbound' at Sarah Fletcher's grave, so he introduced himself and offered to relate her tragic history. This is what he told Mrs ffoulkes:

'Sarah Fletcher and her husband, Captain Fletcher, lived at **Clifton Hampden** not far from here. Captain Fletcher was in the Navy and, following the popular traditions of the sea, he was not only inconstant but unfaithful. He actually proposed marriage to a wealthy heiress living some distance away, and he was on the point of committing bigamy when Mrs Fletcher, warned at the last moment, had only just time to reach the church and stop the ceremony. It is not difficult to imagine the scene which followed. Captain Fletcher literally ran away, made for London, and sailed for the East Indies, the unwedded bride returned home with her parents, and Sarah Fletcher went back to Clifton Hampden and hanged herself in her bedroom, fastening her pocket-handkerchief to a piece of cord which she fixed to the curtain-rod of her bedstead.'

After telling this sad story, the vicar added that the house afterwards gained the reputation of being haunted. Maude ffoulkes now became even more fascinated. Learning that Sarah's former home – Courtiers, a Grade II listed Georgian house in Clifton Hampden – was then being used as a girls' school, she pretended to have an interest in education rather than spooks and was grudgingly shown round by a matron. While she was waiting for the matron to become available, she had an eerie experience. In *True Ghost Stories* she writes: 'I distinctly saw a woman wearing a black cloak looking at me in the shadows of the passageway, whose white face and anguished eyes were crowned with a tangle of auburn curls intertwined with coloured ribbon … then "it" disappeared.'

The entrance to Dorchester Abbey Church, photographed at about the time Maude ffoulkes came upon the memorial to Sarah Fletcher in the graveyard.
©R Holland

The Revd Poyntz put Mrs ffoulkes in touch with a friend, a Revd Edward Crake, who had lived at Courtiers for many years. The Revd Crake had much to tell her. He told her he had moved to Courtiers at the age of ten, with his parents, who ran a prep school in the house. He continued: 'Seven years passed, and I had arrived at the impressionable age of seventeen ... I was a healthy, normal boy, and, as my father had strictly forbidden any gossip likely to prejudice the school, I knew nothing about the tragedy of Sarah Fletcher until the night when she made her presence known, and – let me confess it – I fell in love with her. 'One moonlight night I lay awake in my bedroom, when I heard steps descending the stairs. The door opened, and the unseen walker entered – hesitated, and went out – I lay curious and speculative, until the sound of the church clock striking three set the air vibrating – but, as I heard nothing more, I turned over and went to sleep. The next night the same thing happened: I felt there to be something uncommon about these footsteps, so on the following night I determined to lie in bed with my door open and see for myself what or who came down the stairs. I had not long to wait – the footsteps of someone wearing high-heeled shoes came into the room towards my bed ... then retreated.

'I sprang up, and ran into the long corridor – as bright as day in the white radiance of the moon. Then she was made manifest – and I saw Sarah Fletcher standing by one of the long windows. She seemed tremendously alive. There was nothing "dead" about her; her eyes were full of tears, she had come from the edge of the world, and from soundless space, to seek my love and pity. I was not in the least frightened. I wanted to help her, to befriend her – then all at once a patch of moonlight alone marked the place where she had stood.'

At this point Mrs ffoulkes asked the Revd Crake to describe the ghost.

'She wore a black silk cloak, fashionable at that period for protecting ladies' dresses from the dust of the roads ... she was hatless, and her hair was twined about with a purple-red ribbon, most probably as on the morning when she rushed across the countryside, broken-hearted and desperate.'

Discreetly relating his experience to an assistant master, he learnt that he had discovered the secret shared by all the adult inmates of the house: that ghostly footsteps had frequently been heard coming out of the room where Sarah Fletcher had hanged herself and into Crake's bedroom. Previously, he had slept through the phenomenon. On a subsequent night, he and the teacher he had taken into his confidence sat up in the hope of seeing Sarah's ghost again, and they were not disappointed.

'This time she smiled at me,' said the Revd Crake, 'and her face had lost something of its tragic intensity; she turned the handle of the door, opened it, and I ran towards her. "Speak to me," I begged, "please, please, speak to me" ... but the door closed in my face, and when I pushed it open the room was empty, except for a few boys sleeping quietly, unconscious of the phantom which had passed by.'

The haunting continued off and on for the next ten years. During a particularly active period, Edward Crake was asked to return to Courtiers. The household had been disturbed not only by the sound of footsteps but also by 'frantic knockings', the opening and closing of doors by unseen hands and the ringing of a bell. The newly ordained Revd Crake attempted an exorcism. He saw the ghost of Sarah Fletcher one last time but his attempt at an exorcism was only partially successful. The disturbances continued, though less frantically, but the school was removed from Clifton Hampden and housed elsewhere. That was the end of the Revd Crake's romance with this sorrowful spirit of the 18th century and of Mrs ffoulkes's investigations, too.

An artist's representation of Sarah Fletcher's face, based on the sightings of her ghost by Maude ffoulkes and Edward Crake, reproduced in True Ghost Stories.
©R Holland

THE STORY OF AMY ROBSART

In the Middle Ages the Abbey at Abingdon possessed a magnificent grange at Cumnor, a village a few miles west of Oxford. After the Dissolution of the Monasteries in the 16th century, the grange became a country house and was known at various times as Cumnor Place or Cumnor Hall. During the reign of Elizabeth I Cumnor Hall became the centre of a scandal which affected even the queen.

At the time, Elizabeth's favourite was the dashing Sir Robert Dudley. Dudley was a married man but for some years his wife, Amy (née Robsart), had been unwell and rumour had it that, should she die, he would become more than just the favourite of Good Queen Bess. The rumour was supported by the fact that the Queen consistently refused the offers of marriage from numerous foreign nobility, and was further fuelled by the lack of attention Dudley paid to his wife, who never came to court and instead carried out a rather lonely existence in one or other of the houses belonging to her husband or her own family. In 1560, while Lady Dudley was staying at Cumnor Hall, tragedy struck. As John Ingram explains in his *Haunted Homes and Family Legends of Great Britain* (1884):

'According to the evidence given to the Coroner, Lady Dudley, on Sunday, the 8th of September, 1560, had ordered all her household to go to a fair then being held at Abingdon. Mrs Odingsell, her companion, had remonstrated with her for this order, observing that the day was not a proper one for decent folks to go to a fair; whereupon her Ladyship grew very angry, and said, "All *her* people should go." And they went, leaving only Lady Dudley and two other women in the house. Upon their return the unfortunate lady was found dead at the bottom of a flight of stairs, but whether fallen by accident, or through suicide, or flung there by assassins, is, seemingly, an unfathomable mystery.'

Although Lord Dudley had been away at court, and the inquest ruled the death an accident, the rumour mill now went into overdrive. The death of poor Amy Robsart was just too convenient, it seemed, and would now pave the way for Dudley to marry the Queen. One of his henchmen, Sir Richard Verney, who had been at Cumnor at the time, later came under the spotlight as the possible assassin but no wrongdoing has ever been substantiated and the opinion of modern historians tends away from the murder theory. Unfortunately for Dudley, the rumours made it impossible for Queen Elizabeth to marry him, for this would implicate Her Majesty in the scandal. She retained him as a favourite, however, and a few years later made him Earl of Leicester. That she was in love with him might perhaps be inferred from the fact that Elizabeth remained the Virgin Queen for the rest of her life.

Whatever the Coroner and the Queen thought about Lady Dudley's death, the people of Cumnor felt they knew better: she did not fall, she was pushed. When tales got about that the lady's ghost was haunting the hall and its grounds, it was all the proof they needed of Dudley's supposed crime. The spirit of a murder victim could not be expected to lie easy in its grave, they asserted.

Tradition states that 'nine parsons from Oxford' were brought in to exorcise Lady Dudley's ghost and they 'laid it' (as the terminology has it) in a body of water which for years afterwards bore the name of 'Madam Dudley's Pond'. This pond was never known to freeze, which the country folk took as evidence of 'Madam Dudley's' presence within it. Nevertheless, there continued to be reports of her ghost being seen, especially after a popular ballad by the 18th-century poet William Mickle and later a novel by Sir Walter Scott both highlighted the murder theory in a fanciful and sensational manner. By this time Cumnor Hall had become little more than a ruin (it has long since been demolished entirely). The site, not far from the village church, was avoided as a cursed place for many long years, however. As Mickle puts it:

The village maids, with fearful glance,
Avoid the ancient mossgrown wall;
Nor ever lead the merry dance,
Among the groves of Cumnor Hall.

There is also a tradition of Amy Robsart's ghost appearing, just once, at **Cornbury Park**, a stately home near Charlbury. While Lord Dudley was hunting in Wychwood Forest, his dead wife's spirit manifested in front of him and warned him to prepare himself, for he would be dead within ten days. She was right. On September 4, 1588, Lord Dudley died, some believed by poison.

This illustration of Cumnor Hall forms the frontispiece of the 1912 illustrated edition of John Ingram's Haunted Homes and Family Legends of Great Britain.
© R Holland

THE TANFIELDS AND THE WILCOTES

Sir Laurence and Lady Tanfield must have been notorious characters for they feature strongly in the folklore of **Burford** and the surrounding villages as somewhat assertive ghosts. Sir Laurence was a wealthy judge who bought Burford Priory in the early 17th century. Using his knowledge of the law, it is said, Sir Laurence found ways of cheating his neighbours to his own advantage. His wife was no more popular. She held the district in contempt, on one occasion declaring that she 'would like to grind the people of Burford to powder beneath her chariot wheels'. According to traditional ghost-lore, such wickedness tends to bind haughty aristocrats to the earth after death and the Tanfields were no exception. Their ghosts had the habit of riding round the town in a fiery coach, often in the air, over the roofs of the houses.

The townsfolk had had quite enough of the Tanfields when they were alive and they weren't prepared to put up with any more bad behaviour now they were dead. They gathered together seven clergymen to exorcise them. The unruly spirits were trapped in bottles and 'laid' under Burford Bridge. There they are trapped till doomsday, unless the arch below which the bottles were buried should ever run dry. During an unusually dry summer one year, the water sank very low and it began to 'hiss and bubble' in an alarming manner. The town mobilised and everyone poured fresh water under the bridge to make sure it didn't dry up completely.

*The Cotswolds town of Burford was formerly terrorised by the aggressive
ghosts of Lord and Lady Tanfield.*
stocker1970/ShutterStock

Lord and Lady Wilcote must have been even more wicked than
the Tanfields, for they died way back in the 15th century but
their memory lived on with equal disfavour in the folklore of the
neighbouring villages of **Wilcote** and **North Leigh**.
Nevertheless, it has been quite forgotten what they did to make
themselves so unpopular. Like the Tanfields, Lord and Lady
Wilcote's ghosts had the habit of riding around in an airborne
phantom coach. According to an account collected by folklorist
Violet Hunt, 'they got so strong they could be seen in full
daylight'. The ghosts were finally defeated by seven clergyman
(another account says twelve). The spirit of Lord Wilcote told
the exorcists he would continue to haunt 'as long as the clapper

and the bell hang together'. This bizarre statement led to the removal and melting down of Wilcote's church bell. It and the ghosts were laid together in a pond at Wilcote.

The Wilcotes' mortal remains are buried at North Leigh and there is a splendid memorial to them in the church. The marble effigy of Lady Wilcote shows her lying with her hands together as if in prayer. They are not quite touching. Perhaps it is resentment towards whatever wrongs she was perceived as committing during her lifetime, but legend has it this pious attitude is a hollow one and that, by some supernatural agency, her stone hands are slowly pulling apart. When they have fallen entirely apart, states the tradition, her ghost will return.

THE GRAND HOUSES

Blenheim Palace is Oxfordshire's grandest stately home, a vast building standing among formal gardens and 2,000 acres of parkland designed by Capability Brown. Blenheim was constructed in the early 18th century on the orders of the First Duke of Marlborough, replacing an earlier mansion, Woodstock Manor (or Palace), of which only one stone remains. It is famous today for being the birthplace of Winston Churchill and for the extraordinary collection of antiques and works of art on show in its state rooms. Blenheim Palace is still privately owned but is open to the public.

The magnificent frontage of Blenheim Palace, the Vanbrugh-designed mansion which replaced the medieval Woodstock Manor in the 18th century.
Reproduced with the kind permission of Blenheim Palace

According to *Paranormal Oxford* by Ross Andrews, the Dean Jones Room is haunted by the man after whom it is named, the First Duke of Marlborough's chaplain. The author states that in addition the ghost of a Roundhead haunts one of the bedrooms, despite the fact that Blenheim post-dates the Civil War. Perhaps this is a case of mistaken identity. At any rate, his is a quiet ghost, who sits attempting to warm himself in front of the fire.

A well-known and much discussed haunting occurred at Woodstock Manor at the height of the Civil War, in 1649. Having wrested the manor from Royalist forces, Parliamentary Commissioners moved in. King Charles himself had used Woodstock as a base for a while, so it was a matter of pride for the Roundheads that it had now come under their control. According to one George Sinclair, who wrote about the incident in 1685, they made use of the King's own suite of rooms, turning his bedroom into a kitchen and the former Royalist Council Room into a brewery. They also hacked down a magnificent oak tree in the grounds because it was called the King's Oak and chopped it up for firewood. It was after this outrage that the house suddenly became possessed of what today we would call a poltergeist but which the Puritan Parliamentarians dubbed 'the Royalist Devil'. The folklorist Christina Hole explained what happened in her seminal work on *Haunted England* (1941):

'On October 16th two Commissioners and their servants saw what they took to be a dog entering the room and gnawing the cords under their beds; on the following night the beds were so violently hoisted up and let down again by invisible hands that the sleepers were badly bruised. The wood from the King's Oak was found strewn about and the chairs and stools were overturned. From that time forward disturbances occurred every night. Trenchers, stones, horse-bones and glass were hurled about the rooms; candles were blown out as soon as they were lighted, bedclothes and curtains were torn from the beds. On one occasion the servants were drenched with "stinking Ditch-water"; on another, "glass flew about so thick (and yet not one of the Chamber windows was broken) that they thought it had rained money. Whereupon they lighted candles, but to their grief they found nothing but glass."

'On October 29th the walls were shaken and the windows broken by loud and persistent noises which were heard by all the neighbours and so terrified the servants that one man nearly killed a companion whom he took for the spirit. Similar sounds were heard on November 2nd, this time in three different places, so that "the very Rabbet Stealers, who were abroad that night, were so affrighted by the dismal Thundering, that for haste they left their Ferrets in the holes behind them". On the same night one of the Roundheads saw a hoof kicking out the candle, but when he tried to strike it with his sword, invisible hands tore the weapon from him and stunned him with a blow. After that the Commissioners gave up their unequal contest and left the place, and the Royalist Devil was heard of no more.'

So, was a poltergeist, angry spirit or devil responsible or were all the disturbances down merely to a gang of Royalist supporters pulling a few scary stunts, leaving imagination and mass hysteria to do the rest? To this day no one is quite sure what happened at Woodstock Manor during that dramatic autumn of 1649.

The legend of 'Fair Rosamund' is also associated with Woodstock Manor. Rosamund was mistress to King Henry II. Henry's queen, the fiery Eleanor of Aquitaine, was less than pleased with this infatuation so he kept Rosamund out of sight in various shelters in the garden. A silver thread would be laid by trusted guards every night to lead the king to the 'bower' where Rosamund was waiting to meet him. When the king was away one night, however, it was Eleanor who found her way to the bower; and she forced her hated rival to drink poison. The ghost of 'Fair Rosamund' may be the ghostly lady in white said to occasionally be seen in Blenheim's restaurant kitchens. She is also said to haunt the ruins of nearby Godstow Nunnery and the Trout Inn (see the 'Haunted Hostelries' chapter). A spring called 'Rosamund's Well' can still be seen in the grounds of Blenheim Palace.

Stonor Park is another splendid manor house, one of the first in England to be built of brick. It boasts a particularly lovely setting among the Chiltern Hills. The family seat of the Stonor family and Baron Camoys, Stonor Park has been in the Stonor family for more than eight centuries. It is a very ancient site. Quite apart from the 12th-century chapel incorporated into the 16th-century main house, there is a prehistoric stone circle in the grounds: it's quite possible Stonor got its name from this monument. The house and its famous deer park are open to the public.

The historic and beautifully situated Stonor Park, a place of 'many strange things'.

Author Antony Hippisley Coxe learnt of 'many strange things' happening at Stonor Park. The heavy tread of someone invisible has been heard walking across a landing, down a flight of stairs to a room where the door of a cupboard inexplicably opens. Some have also heard the muffled sounds of conversation emanating from empty rooms and one or two people have reported the disturbing experience of having their faces felt by an unseen hand as they lie in their beds.

The ghosts are not confined to the house. According to Hippisley Coxe, dogs have been known to behave strangely in the garden behind the house. They apparently see something humans cannot see; and whatever it is, they don't like it, for they tend to back away snarling. Even the stone circle may be haunted, for a 'curious animal smell' has been detected here which no one can explain.

Hippisley Coxe also states that '**Shipton Court** had a ghost who was exorcised and the haunted room sealed up. No one knows where this room is.' Shipton Court is a 17th-century house built of mellow Cotswold Stone and now offers holiday accommodation. Hippisley Coxe does not give a source for his assertion regarding the haunted room, so the likelihood of it having been incorporated into any of the rented apartments is open to conjecture. The author also mentions that **Bruern Abbey** is haunted by a phantom monk. There is little trace of the original Benedictine abbey, for it was replaced by a Georgian manor house (now a boys' school). Indeed the ghostly monk is one of the few remnants: he takes a four-mile walk from Bruern Abbey to Tangley Hall, following the route of a subterranean tunnel below his sandalled feet.

Stanton Harcourt Manor is a private home situated at the centre of the village. The poet Alexander Pope lived here in the 1780s, translating Homer's *Iliad*, and in a window in the tower he scratched a message of celebration on completing the task. Until it was exorcised, the manor house was haunted by Dame Alice Harcourt who, legend has it, was murdered while the rest of her family were at prayer, her dismembered body then being lobbed out of a window. Unfortunately, no explanation is forthcoming for this horrible deed. Her restless spirit was laid in a nearby pond, which later became known as Lady Pool. She shares this watery bed with a Mrs Hall, who killed herself in the

18th century after discovering that her husband was having an affair. Her spirit too was exorcised to Lady Pool but it is said that should the pond ever dry up, both women will return to haunt the village.

The Grey Lady of **Horspath Manor House** is another murder victim. She was killed by her husband, who then tried to cover up the crime by hiding the body in a priest hole. His unfortunate wife's spirit is said to still wander the landing and also the grounds of the manor house. In 1878 a guest in the house decided to stake out the Grey Lady; when he saw her, he whipped out his pistol and shot the harmless spook three times (as if she hadn't suffered enough in life!). The Grey Lady not unnaturally vanished and the next morning three bullet holes were found in the wall behind where the apparition had been standing.

The original **Holton Park** was demolished in the early 1800s and replaced with a much smaller house. This has now been converted into a school. According to one authority, the first house was knocked down because it was so badly haunted. However, the newer house also has its ghosts. One of these is a former nanny who tripped on the stairs while carrying a baby in her arms. She fell and the baby was killed. Full of remorse, her unhappy spirit continued to haunt Holton Park.

The other ghost has also been seen on the staircase: a small boy dressed in blue velvet. He is supposed to have been an heir to the estate who was murdered by his guardian and governess. The murder took place in the old house but the ghost moved to the Georgian one. Cecil Tyndale-Biscoe, who went on to become a missionary in Kashmir, was one of those who saw the boy in blue. He was only a boy himself when he saw the apparition 'hurtling down the stairs'. Astonished to see this young stranger in his home, Cecil tried to stop him but the boy deftly dodged past him and headed into the hall. Turning to run after him, Mr Tyndale-Biscoe then saw the intruder 'go up suddenly in smoke as if he had exploded'.

One more murder is recalled in the gruesome apparition said to be seen at **Mapledurham House**. The story goes that a former master of Mapledurham killed one of his servants in a fit of temper and he is still to be seen dragging the body of his victim along the floor. Mapledurham House, together with its historic mill (the last one still working on the Thames), is open to the public at summer weekends and on Bank Holidays.

A phantom coach and horses has been seen 'careering silently' across the courtyard of **Weston Manor** at Weston-on-the-Green, now a country house hotel. The tower is said to be haunted by a dairymaid who threw herself from the roof, possibly because she had been seduced by a former owner. Inside the hotel one of the rooms has been dubbed 'Maude's Room' and people staying here, including a newspaper reporter, have experienced disturbed nights. The main phenomenon is an unaccountable rise in temperature – a complete contrast to the sudden chills more commonly associated with ghosts.

Tradition states that 'Mad Maude' was a nun who had an illicit affair with a monk. When the affair came to light, Maude was burned at the stake. 'Maude's Room' – more properly the Oak Room – is believed to incorporate the former monk's cell in which she was caught *in flagrante delicto*. This handsome 14th-century mansion started life as a monastery. The journalist who stayed in the room in order to write a feature for her newspaper reported: 'I cannot remember, even in Africa, such a close and oppressive atmosphere. I was not only hot but unable to breathe properly. Strangely, as daylight filled the room, the temperature dropped.'

Minster Lovell Hall is a beautiful but at times undeniably creepy place: the ruins of a manor house dating from the 15th century, standing near the church beside the River Windrush. It is now in the care of English Heritage. It was the home of Lord Lovell, described as 'Richard III's henchman'. During the War of the Roses, Lord Lovell chose to support the Yorkists, which initially proved a smart move, for subsequent royal favours made him one of the richest men in England. Unfortunately, the tide turned very much against him after the Battle of Bosworth and during the reign of Henry VII he went into hiding. He was never heard of again. The solution to this historical mystery may have been found thanks to an extraordinary and rather grisly discovery in 1708, when renovations were being carried out at the hall. Workmen uncovered a secret room in the basement and within it there was the skeleton of a man, sitting at a table, with the crumbling remains of a book, paper and a pen in front of him. This surely was the missing Lord Lovell!

Eerie groans emanating from the ground are presumed to belong to the unfortunate Lord Lovell, as are the disembodied footsteps that pace the ruins and the apparition which has occasionally been spotted of 'the figure of a tall man in what looks like a cloak'.

The romantic and eerie ruins of Minster Lovell Hall, haunt of a medieval Lord Lovell and a woman in white.
OneToRemember/ShutterStock

Minster Lovell Hall is also claimed as one of a number of locations where a widespread ghostly legend is claimed as having originally taken place. This is the story of 'The Mistletoe Bough'. Once upon a time it was the tradition for a bride to coyly hide on her wedding day. The groom's friends would then make a search and, having found the blushing young woman, pretend to capture her and take her, as if unwillingly, to church. The custom of the groom or his friends 'stealing' the bride from her parents' house dates back thousands of years, even to pre-Hellenic Greece. Unfortunately, in the tale of 'The Mistletoe Bough', the bride hides far too well: she conceals herself in an old chest or coffer in the attic, the lid locks shut, she is unable to open it again and suffocates. Her disappearance remains a mystery for many, many years until the chest is opened again and the poor bride's skeletal body is found within, enshrouded in her white wedding gown.

After the discovery, the bride tends to haunt the house of her sad demise, as a 'White Lady'. The ruins of Minster Lovell Hall are indeed haunted by a White Lady, as Betty Puttick notes in her *Oxfordshire Stories of the Supernatural*:

'In September 1993 a local Witney resident and his friend visited the hall one evening and as they walked through the ruins they suddenly saw the white lady, later describing her as a young girl in her teens wearing a long white gown, a wreath of flowers on her long dark hair. She was in what would have been the main chamber and they watched as she mounted invisible stairs and on reaching a height of about fifteen feet she suddenly disappeared.'

Betty Puttick adds the interesting detail that the chest in which the girl is said to have met her tragic end is now in Greys Court, near Henley-on-Thames; a house that formerly belonged to the Lovell family and which is now in the care of the National Trust.

HAUNTED HOLY PLACES

Rycote Chapel is the only survivor of Rycote Palace, which was built by Richard Quatremayne in the 15th century. It is one of the few churches in the care of English Heritage, this special status granted because of its beautiful interior, which boasts among other splendours an exquisitely carved rood screen and a minstrels' gallery. It was originally the private chapel of Rycote Palace, the rest of the house being destroyed by fire in the middle of the 18th century. It was then the home of a Lord Williams and it is believed one of his female relatives died in the blaze. Some say it is her ghost that has been glimpsed in the chapel.

Known as the 'Grey Lady', she is said to glide out of one of the old family pews, cross the chapel and then vanish through a blocked-up doorway which originally led into the grand house's living quarters. However, in the 1960s, one of Rycote Chapel's custodians, a Mr Clifford Morris, saw a woman in grey outside the chapel, coming towards it from the site of the Palace. He knew she was a ghost for she was dressed in the costume of the Tudor period.

He told ghost-hunter, the late Andrew Green: 'She was tall and slim and was wearing a pale grey gown which had a sheen, rather like satin. She also wore a flowing veil attached to a circular, closely-fitted head-dress.'

It was the afternoon and Mr Morris had a clear view of the apparition as it crossed over the lawn before suddenly disappearing beneath a big yew tree. Are there two Grey Ladies at Rycote or just the one, haunting both the chapel and the grounds?

The story behind the headless ghost of **Faringdon** churchyard is a confused one, the legend largely failing to tally with what little historical fact can be gathered. In the *Ingoldsby Legends*, that odd jumble of traditional yarns and tall tales collected by Richard Harris Barham during the 1830s, it is called 'The Legend of Hamilton Tighe'. In this version, Hamilton is the oldest son by a previous marriage who is standing in the way of an inheritance which would otherwise come to the son of his wicked stepmother. When Hamilton goes to fight the Spanish as a naval officer, his stepmother bribes the captain of his ship to make sure he doesn't return. The captain rather enterprisingly shoves Hamilton into the path of a Spanish cannonball, and it knocks his head from his shoulders. Later, as the wicked stepmum and the favoured son are travelling to church for Hamilton's memorial service, his ghost appears before them, his head tucked underneath his arm. The shock of this sends the stepmother off her own head and she breaks down and confesses all.

So much for the legend. The scanty facts that can be pieced together suggest that the young man who inspired the story was actually called Hampden Pye. He was the oldest son of Sir Robert Pye, a Cromwellian who besieged his Royalist father's house at Faringdon, and Anne Hampden, daughter of a senior Roundhead officer. It is said the young Hampden Pye was something of a reprobate and his parents tended to favour their steady middle son, Edmund. When it was discovered Hampden had married a barmaid, his parents forced him to join the Navy and he was killed in a battle in 1702 (a year after both parents died).

According to tradition, Hampden/Hamilton's headless ghost haunted the churchyard at Faringdon for many years after his death. Eventually the vicar succeeded in pacifying the angry spirit with bell, book and candle and he went at last to his rest.

At **Burford**, the Priory and Old Rectory are both haunted. The Priory is an Elizabethan manor house built on the site of a medieval Augustinian priory. As well as being the former home of the 'wicked' Lord Tanfield (see 'The Tanfields and the Wilcotes' chapter), two kings have slept here, Charles II (with his mistress Nell Gwyn) and James I. In 1947 the mansion returned to being a religious house, with twenty or so nuns of the Benedictine order living here in quiet contemplation. At that time the Old Rectory accommodated the chaplain and staff. Forty years later they became private homes again.

A 'little brown monk' is the ghost of Burford Priory. He has often been seen standing in the entrance hall and sometimes in the chapel, as well as shuffling along the path between the two. Odd noises have also been reported, including footsteps and a knocking on doors and walls. Strangest of all is the invisible bell that occasionally rings in the house, always at two o'clock in the morning, corresponding with one of the many calls to prayer expected of the Augustinian monks.

*John Leech's illustration of Hamilton Tighe from a Victorian edition
of Ingoldsby Legends.*
© R Holland

At the handsome Old Rectory, faced with Cotswold Stone, there is a ghostly gamekeeper, patrolling the grounds with an old-fashioned gun under his arm. Soft singing or chanting has been heard in the garden. Centuries ago this was the burial ground for the monks in the medieval Priory. Poltergeist activity has been reported from the house, with objects being hurled by invisible hands or mysteriously vanishing, and an unexplained screaming has been known to emanate from an empty room.

In 1962 the vicarage in **Deddington** allegedly became haunted after the death of the Revd Maurice Frost, who had had lived there for forty years. His cousin, Mr H Campbell Jarrett, arrived from abroad to settle the Revd Frost's affairs and found the servants in a state of dread. Unaccountable spooky phenomena were happening all over the house. Odd noises were heard in empty rooms, including a cough in the drawing room which a servant assumed had been made by Mr Jarrett till she found him upstairs. More disturbing was the weird pressing down on the beds which was felt every morning between eight-thirty and nine o'clock. On one occasion Mr Jarrett found himself prevented from leaving the drawing room by what was described as 'a mysterious hand'. Mr Jarrett believed the disturbances were down to his deceased cousin, who simply couldn't bear to be separated from his books and his collection of antique clocks.

HAUNTED HOSTELRIES

As a boy first reading up on the subject of ghosts, I was startled to see in the book I was reading (*Discovering Ghosts* by Leon Metcalfe) a story entitled 'The Leper in the Birdcage'. The image conjured up in my over-ripe imagination by this title is better not revisited. I'm not sure whether I was relieved or disappointed to discover The Birdcage was the name of a pub. Oxfordshire has a wealth of haunted pubs and inns and The Birdcage in **Thame** is one of the best known.

Eerie footsteps and mysterious knockings have been heard in The Birdcage. Centuries ago this half-timbered building was a Market House where trade was administered. It was known then as The Cage but in the 16th century it was bought by a Mr Bird, and so became Bird's Cage. There is a tradition that at about this time lepers lived in a top-floor room, kept isolated from their fellow citizens for fear of contagion (although we know today that leprosy is barely contagious).

In the 1970s, the landlady's children were often disturbed by the knocking and two guests saw and felt something ghostly, 'a sort of cold mist drifting out of the [bedroom] door'. A team of psychic investigators held a seance in a top-floor room and, using the time-honoured 'knock once for yes, twice for no' technique, asked the spirit what it wanted. 'Kill you' was the less than encouraging reply. A few days later the landlady attempted a friendly, if one-sided, chat with the supposed ghost and the phenomena calmed down. Today odd things still occur from time to time, including scratching sounds, cold spots and the glimpsing of flitting shadows in the bar.

The equally old-world Bull Inn on Bell Street, **Henley-on-Thames**, has a subtle and enigmatic haunting: the aroma of burnt candles in one area of the bar. A clue perhaps to this phenomenon is the ghostly monk that occasionally manifests in one of the bedrooms. His cowled form has been known to peer down at guests as they lie in bed. Candles and a monk suggest a religious aspect to the haunting and it's possible that at some point in the early life of this venerable building it had an ecclesiastical use.

The handsome Bear Hotel in **Woodstock** dates all the way back to the 12th century. One of the rooms in the hotel has a haunted reputation. Objects have been moved about, lights switched on by invisible hands and disembodied footsteps have been heard to make their way across the creaking floorboards. The phenomena usually occur at about 3am. The

A satirical cartoon lampooning the 'Royalist Devil' events in Woodstock Manor in 1649.

eerie sounds of a baby crying have also been reported. It is said that centuries ago a child was born, illegitimately, to a servant girl and to avoid any scandal she stuffed the infant into a chimney to suffocate it and to hide its tiny corpse. A phantom woman in black has been seen in the early hours of the morning and she may perhaps be the ghost of the cruel mother.

The Crown at **Pishill** is a striking-looking old hostelry with a rather Gothic appearance. The apparition seen here is a dark figure wrapped in a black cloak. In the days of the Catholic persecution, a priest had hidden in The Crown but one night he almost literally stumbled into a charming barmaid at the inn and, despite his vows of chastity, fell immediately in love with her. Not long after, he was lying up in his secret hiding place when he overheard his beloved being roundly insulted by a haughty aristocratic customer. Unable to contain his rage, the priest suddenly burst onto the scene and furiously defended his lady's honour. The result was that he and the customer fought a duel. Predictably, it was the holy man rather than the experienced swordsman who lost his life and it is he who now haunts the pub.

A priest also haunts the grand Whately Hall Hotel in **Banbury**. His name was Father Bernard and he was one among a number of Catholics who used a room here to practise their faith. It had been arranged that a bell was to be rung as a warning should investigators suddenly turn up, giving them time to escape through a secret tunnel. One night a silly young servant decided to ring the bell for a joke. The shock and stress caused Father Bernard to suffer a fatal heart attack as he was trying to make his unnecessary escape.

The ghost of the medieval White Hart in **Minster Lovell** is another in quite a series of Oxfordshire hostelries to be haunted by women in distress. She is seen sobbing her heart out behind a veil she wears to cover her face. For time immemorial she has been known as 'Rosalind'. It is believed that after a failed love affair Rosalind hanged herself from a spiral staircase. Her unhappy apparition tends to be seen in the place where this staircase, long since removed, formerly stood. Odd incidents, like the dropping of a hand-bell onto the floor and the inexplicable smashing of glasses, have also been blamed on Rosalind.

The George Inn at **Wallingford** is also haunted by a weeping woman. Her story, too, is tragic. She watched her lover being killed in a brawl and the sight of it drove her mad. She mixed her tears with soot from the fire and with her finger drew great black teardrops on the room which she now haunts (and which from then on was known as the Teardrop Room).

There is no story to explain the sad-looking spectral woman haunting the George Hotel at **Dorchester**. Dressed all in white, she is said to

The George Inn, Dorchester, photographed just prior to the First World War. The George is one of Oxfordshire's many historic and haunted inns.

creep through the hotel and into one room where she stands staring forlornly at a four-poster bed. Perhaps she was a jilted bride, disappointed that after all she would have to sleep alone.

The ghostly woman at the Holt Hotel, **Steeple Aston**, dresses in black rather than white and she is seen carrying a baby, whom it is believed she fatally neglected, later being charged for its murder. In addition to the hotel itself she has been encountered on the road outside. The Holt Hotel has another ghost, that of the handsome highwayman Claude Duval, who enjoyed spending his loot here.

The spook at The Red Lion in **Kidlington** is believed to be the angry spirit of a woman who died in a fire at the old pub on the site. The current premises is a pizza bar but it's more than pizza dough that's being tossed in the air here: the ghost's main trick is throwing things around, mainly in the kitchen and a bathroom.

The most famous female phantom associated with an Oxfordshire pub must surely be 'Fair Rosamund', the mistress of King Henry II, whom we encountered in the 'Grand Houses' chapter. Her lovely form is said to not only flit among the ruins of Godstow Nunnery, **Wolvercote**, where was buried, but more often – sensible ghost – in the more welcoming environs of the Trout Inn, which stands nearby. Fair though she was in life, as a ghost Rosamund can behave badly, disturbing the furniture and knocking over glasses and bottles as well as suddenly appearing in front of startled diners. In some parts of the inn it looks as if she is walking on her knees. This is because the floor level has been raised so much since her day that her feet are now obscured. Other phenomena reported from the Trout include a rather unnerving whispering in the ears and an inexplicable aroma of flowers. Rosamund is said to have been buried with a sprig of heather, so the scent may be an echo of this.

GHOSTS ABROAD

Standing surrounded by rusting railings in a field near **Ipsden** can be found a small ivy-clad obelisk with a pyramidal top. This is a memorial to a young man named John Thurlow Reade, who lived at Ipsden House, about half a mile away, in the early 19th century. The monument was put up by John's oldest brother Edward (another brother was the historical novelist Charles Reade) and includes the date of his death, 'November 25 AD 1827', and the place where he died, 'Sehaaranpore'. John worked for the East India Company and at the time of his death was stationed at Saharanpur in Uttar Pradesh.

An affectionate son, he wrote regularly to his mother, who would often walk down to the Wallingford road in order to pick up the post directly from the carrier. There came a lengthy stretch in which no letters came from John, and Mrs Reade began to worry. Then, one morning, she got a presentiment that if she walked down to the road again, news of her son would come. She set off as usual but only got half way. Near where the memorial now stands, she suddenly saw a vision of John. He appeared to be in great distress and desperately trying to tell his mother something important – then he vanished.

Soon word came from his employers that John had died on the day Mrs Reade had seen the apparition and that he had been buried by his Indian servants. Mrs Reade was convinced he had not been given a proper Christian burial, and that his spirit had attempted to tell her so. At her request, the vicar of St Mary's Church in Ipsden held a burial service for John Reade. Some years later Edward raised the memorial to his brother close to where his mother had seemingly encountered his troubled spirit.

There are a number of other examples of ghosts being encountered in the Oxfordshire countryside. **Watch Folly**, a low hill above Ipsden, for example, is haunted by a shepherd boy who surprised a gang of sheep stealers and was hanged by them from an oak tree on the summit. Not far away, at **Witheridge Hill**, near Stoke Row, 'a ghostly woman, sitting and brooding', has been seen beside a stone wall in a wood.

Most of these outdoors ghosts are encountered on Oxfordshire's roads. The apparition of a highwayman, known locally as 'Blackstockings' because of his fancy leg-wear, gallops along the B4047 near the hamlet of **Worsham**, Minster Lovell. Other than this odd detail of dress, he is every inch the highwayman of tradition: black horse, black cloak, tricorn hat, mask and a threateningly brandished flintlock pistol. Another phantom horseman, rarely seen but sometimes heard, thunders through the village of **Hempton**. His identity is unknown. On lanes around the village 'an elemental force' has the unpleasant habit of knocking cyclists off their bikes. Even weirder is the mysterious black cloud occasionally encountered on the roads around **Burford**. 'If you drive through it,' writes Antony Hippisley Coxe, 'you experience a feeling of utter terror. Animals are driven frantic.'

A horse without a rider has been seen galloping at night on a road leading into **Denchworth**. Apparently in a state of panic, the phantom animal veers from side to side in the road before abruptly disappearing. At **Charlbury** a 'huge white stallion' startles motorists by leaping over high hedges and into the road in front of them. One witness saw it effortlessly clear a seven-foot-high hedge. The road between Charlbury and **Finstock** is the haunt of a spectral coach-and-four. Sometimes it is seen, sometimes just heard trundling along. On one occasion, it was heard by a woman taking a walk with her little boy but, unlike her, the child was also able to see it. He said it was green and had two men up behind the horses. In it was a sobbing woman, dressed in black and wearing a large, feathered hat. According to the boy, this woman beckoned to him to come closer and looked very angry when his mother led him away.

Motorists really have to be on their guard when driving round the county. Some ghosts seem to be going out of their way to cause accidents. A man wearing a cap and overcoat runs in front of cars on a minor road near **East Hanney**. As the driver slams on the brakes, he vanishes. He is supposedly the apparition of a man who died in an accident here – hardly surprising with that sort of behaviour. A spectral cyclist at **Littlemore** also seems to have a death wish, according to motorists who have encountered it.

Motorists also need to beware on the B4100 at **Souldern**, for a number of witnesses have reported seeing a Morris Traveller driving along here without its headlights. On one occasion a motorcyclist nearly crashed into it. It seems to travel exclusively on foggy nights, the most dangerous conditions possible, and vanishes when a real vehicle approaches. Another mysteriously vanishing car and an equally ghostly gypsy caravan have both been seen on separate occasions near the **Rollright Stones**, a prehistoric stone circle.

Finally, there is the smart red sports car, badly damaged and immobile in the middle of the A4260 between **Banbury** and **Oxford**, which caused witness Sue Ede to brake sharply when it suddenly loomed out of the darkness. The car appeared to be empty as Sue drove slowly past it, so she did not stop, presuming it had been abandoned. Two miles down the road, however, there it was again! It disappeared seconds after the astonished Sue began to slow down. In seeking a solution to this extraordinary experience, Sue learnt that an American had died in a fatal crash in his sports car along that stretch of road some years previously.

Ghostly highwaymen have been reported from Oxfordshire, including one named 'Blackstockings' who gallops along on a black horse near Minster Lovell.

Other **GHOST STORIES** for you to enjoy from
BRADWELL BOOKS

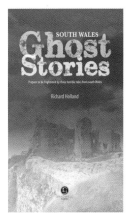

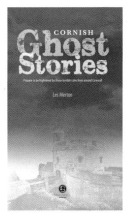

More **GHOST STORIES** from
BRADWELL BOOKS on next page

Black Country & Birmingham
Ghost Stories

Cambridgeshire
Ghost Stories

Cumbrian
Ghost Stories

Derbyshire
Ghost Stories

Leicestershire
Ghost Stories

Scottish
Ghost Stories

BRADWELL
BOOKS